Givens

odoemela 2B

GERALD R.
FORD

PRESIDENTIAL ✦ LEADERS

GERALD R. FORD

MARY MUELLER WINGET

TWENTY-FIRST CENTURY BOOKS/MINNEAPOLIS

To John, my apolitical friend

Twenty-First Century Books
A division of Lerner Publishing Group
241 First Avenue North
Minneapolis, MN 55401 U.S.A.

Website address: www.lernerbooks.com

Library of Congress Cataloging-in-Publication Data

Winget, Mary.
    Gerald R. Ford / by Mary Mueller Winget.
        p.   cm. — (Presidential leaders)
    Includes bibliographical references and index.
    ISBN-13: 978-0-8225-1509-8 (lib. bdg. : alk. paper)
    ISBN-10: 0-8225-1509-1 (lib. bdg. : alk. paper)
    1. Ford, Gerald R., 1913– —Juvenile literature. 2. Presidents—United States—Biography—
Juvenile literature. 3. Vice-Presidents—United States—Biography—Juvenile literature.
4. Legislators—United States—Biography—Juvenile literature. 5. United States. Congress.
House—Biography—Juvenile literature. I. Title. II. Series.
    E866.W56 2007
    973.925092—dc22   2006008282

Manufactured in the United States of America
1 2 3 4 5 6 – JR – 12 11 10 09 08 07

Contents

◇

Gerald R. Ford graduated from South High School in Grand Rapids, Michigan, in 1931.

INTRODUCTION

*No other nation in history has ever dedicated
itself more specifically nor devoted itself more
completely to the proposition that all men are
created equal, that they are endowed by their
Creator with such unalienable rights of life,
liberty and the pursuit of happiness.*
—Gerald R. Ford, July 4, 1976

At South High School in Grand Rapids, Michigan, Gerald
R. Ford played first-string center on the freshman football
team. He was a strong player who became a football star.
He was also a good student. His fellow students liked him
because of his good nature and bright outlook. He always
saw more good things in people than bad things.

In his senior year in 1931, Ford won a contest for the
most popular high school senior in Grand Rapids. The
prize was a trip to Washington, D.C., with thirty other
midwestern seniors. They toured the White House, the
Washington Monument, the Supreme Court, and Congress.
In the House of Representatives, Ford stood in the gallery,

watching members of Congress debating on the floor of the chamber. He never forgot that experience.

Many years later, Gerald R. Ford was elected to Congress from his hometown of Grand Rapids. At that time, his fondest wish was to become Speaker of the House. He wanted that job more than anything. Instead, he became the president of the United States at a critical time in U.S. history.

——————————————— ✧ ———————————————

Ford (bottom center) represented South High School on the 1930 Grand Rapids' All City First Football Team.

CHAPTER ONE

A ROUGH START

*"To know even one life has breathed easier
because you have lived—this is to have
succeeded." Nothing I've ever read sums
up better the credo by which
[my parents] both lived.*
—Gerald R. Ford, 1979

Dorothy Ayer Gardner, Gerald R. Ford's mother, grew up in a happy home in the small town of Harvard, Illinois. Dorothy's father, Levi, owned a furniture store and real estate business. Her mother, Adele Augusta Ayer, was the daughter of one of the town's founding families. Her ancestors were among the New Englanders who founded the United States.

The Gardners sent Dorothy to a small college for women in Knoxville, Illinois. There, in the spring of 1912, she met the brother of her close friend, Marietta King, from Omaha, Nebraska. Although Leslie King was thirty years old, ten years older than Dorothy, they fell in love. After a brief courtship, Leslie convinced Levi Gardner that he had a good job and money in the bank. He would take good care of Dorothy if Levi would allow Leslie to marry his daughter.

Marietta and Leslie's father, Charles Henry King, had made a fortune in railroads. The wedding was a grand affair. Charles King gave the bride and groom a honeymoon train trip that began in the Pacific Northwest and continued down the coast of California. They then traveled to Denver, Colorado, and on to Omaha, Nebraska, where they would live. Not long into the trip, Leslie began striking his wife and calling her insulting names. The couple made up, but five days later, King again began hitting his wife. Instead of the cottage Leslie had promised Dorothy, the newlyweds moved into his parents' mansion. The abuse continued.

Dorothy went home to her parents, but Leslie showed up a few days later. He begged his wife to return. She agreed, and the couple moved into a basement apartment. It was all that Leslie could afford. He had lied about his finances. Around Christmas Dorothy discovered she was pregnant. On Monday, July 14, 1913, the hottest day of the year in Omaha, Dorothy gave birth to a son. Leslie insisted the child be named after him, Leslie Lynch King Jr. The baby was called Junior or Junie.

Sixteen days later, as soon as she was strong enough to travel, Dorothy escaped with her son. She couldn't return to Harvard, Illinois, with a baby and no husband. In those days, it would have shamed both her and her parents. Instead, she moved in with her sister and her husband.

Junie (left)
was baptized in
December 1913.

——————— ✧

They lived in Oak Park, Illinois, a suburb of Chicago. Then she filed for divorce. It was granted on December 19, 1913. The court found Leslie King "guilty of extreme cruelty." It gave "sole custody, care, nurture, training and rearing" of the child to Dorothy.

A NEW START

After the divorce, Dorothy's parents, Levi and Adele, decided to leave Illinois. They moved to Grand Rapids, Michigan, where they owned some land. They bought a nice house at 457 Lafayette Street, and Dorothy and little Junie went to live with them. At the time, Grand Rapids was an up-and-coming community. It was a good place for a child to grow up.

Junie was a lively toddler in 1915.

✧ ——————————————

During her first year in Grand Rapids, 1915, Dorothy went to a social event at Grace Episcopal Church. So did a tall, friendly, dark-haired man named Gerald (Jerry) Rudolf Ford. Jerry had quit school to support his mother and sisters after his father had died in a train accident. He worked hard at his job selling paint and varnish to furniture factories in Grand Rapids. Jerry and Dorothy began dating. She found him to be gentle, respectful, and disciplined. They married on February 1, 1916, at the church where they had first met.

Jerry Ford adopted his stepson, and two-year-old Junie King became Junie Ford. Soon he came to be called Jerry Ford Jr. The relationship between the elder Jerry and his stepson was close and loving. The boy later wrote, "He was the father I grew up to believe was my father, the father I loved and learned from and respected. He was my Dad." The family lived in a rented two-family house on Madison Avenue SE. Jerry attended kindergarten a block and a half from his home. Even at five years old, Jerry played softball and football. He often came home "with a dirty face, torn clothes and skinned knees and elbows."

Dorothy Ford was the strict parent. She soon realized that her son had her first husband's hot temper. Depending on the situation, she reasoned with Jerry, twisted his ear, or sent him to his room. The Fords had three more sons. Tom was born in 1918, Dick in 1924, and Jim in 1927. Their mother supervised the boys' schoolwork and made sure they got to church on Sunday.

Gerald R. Ford Sr. wanted his sons to have the education he never had. He also encouraged them to play sports. Sports, he thought, would help them learn how to compete, to be part of a team, to play by the rules, and to win and lose gracefully. The Fords had three rules: "Tell the truth, work hard, and come to dinner on time—and woe to any of us who violated those rules," Jerry later remembered.

Jerry had his own peculiar method of writing. When he was sitting down, he wrote with his left hand. When he was standing up, he wrote with his right hand. His parents and teachers tried to get him to write only with his right hand. But when he was about ten years old, his parents and teachers finally gave up trying to change his writing habits. They

Jerry (second from left) was a high school freshman in this family photograph taken in October 1927. His brothers sitting beside him are Tom (left) and Dick (right). Jerry Ford Sr. holds baby Jim (front).

———————————— ✧ ————————————

let him use both hands to write. During these years, Jerry also had a problem with stuttering. When he was about ten, the stuttering stopped.

HIGH SCHOOL DAYS

In the spring of 1927, Jerry and one hundred other eighth graders tried out for the football team at South High, where they would be going the next fall. Coach Clifford Gettings chose Jerry to play center. He was a gangly, five-foot-eight-inch kid weighing 130 pounds. Coach Gettings called him Whitey because of his blond hair. Jerry played first-string center on the freshman team. In his sophomore year, he stepped in for the first-team center, who had been injured. Jerry was an aggressive athlete, but in the classroom, he was quiet and well prepared. He struggled with Latin but did well in history and government. In his junior year, he ranked in the top 5 percent of his class and made the National Honor Society.

Throughout high school, Jerry worked at many part-time jobs, from cutting lawns to flipping hamburgers. During this time, he met his birth father, Leslie King, for the first time since 1913. King had remarried. Jerry had a half brother named Leslie and two half sisters named Marjorie and Patricia. But Jerry felt the Fords were his real family.

In his senior year in 1931, Jerry won a trip to Washington, D.C. Standing in the gallery of the House of Representatives, watching members of Congress in action, made a lasting impression on him.

Ford continued to play football in college.

CHAPTER TWO

ON HIS OWN

*If I had to go back to college again—knowing
what I know today—I'd concentrate on two
areas: learning to write and to speak before an
audience. Nothing in life is more important
than the ability to communicate effectively.*
—Gerald R. Ford, 1979

When Jerry Ford Jr. was ready for college in 1931, the
United States was in the midst of the Great Depression
(1929–1942), a time of serious economic trouble around
the globe. Businesses closed, and millions of people lost
their jobs. Gerald Ford Sr. wasn't earning enough money to
help his stepson pay for college. But Arthur Krause, the
principal of South High, decided to step in. Krause started
a scholarship fund with the profits from the school book-
store. Jerry would be the first recipient of the one-hundred-
dollar scholarship—enough to cover tuition for one year at
the University of Michigan at Ann Arbor.

Krause also invited Harry Kipke, the coach of the Michigan football team, to come to Grand Rapids to meet Jerry Ford and his family. Kipke made the trip, saw Jerry play, and invited him to attend the university at Ann Arbor. No football scholarships existed at that time to help pay for Jerry's tuition. But Kipke did find a job for Jerry waiting tables in the university hospital restaurant. An aunt and uncle agreed to send the boy two dollars a week for spending money, and Jerry had saved enough from summer jobs to pay the rent on a third-floor room shared with another student. He showed up in September ready to start a new life.

COLLEGE BOY

Ford, six feet tall and 180 pounds, made first-string center on the freshman football team. He was also doing well in his classes and making friends. Delta Kappa Epsilon, a college fraternity, invited Ford to join. They gave him a job waiting tables at the fraternity house to pay for his room and board. As a fraternity member, Ford made some wealthy friends. New horizons opened to him. That spring he won the Morton Trophy, awarded to the school's outstanding freshman football player.

At the end of his senior year, Ford was voted most valuable player on the squad. He also ranked in the top quarter of his class, majoring in economics and political science. Both the Green Bay Packers and the Detroit Lions offered him twenty-eight hundred dollars to play for them. That was a lot of money in 1935. However, Ford thought that "pro football wouldn't lead me anywhere." He thought he would like to study law, but once again, he had no money.

Ford asked Coach Kipke for a job as an assistant coach after graduation. But Kipke didn't know if there would be an opening. In the meantime, Ducky Pond, the head coach at Yale University in New Haven, Connecticut, was looking for an assistant football coach. Kipke recommended Ford. Pond offered him the job. There was a catch, however. Ford also had to coach the freshman boxing team. Ford knew nothing about boxing. Still he took the job and promised to learn to box.

Before beginning his new life, Ford wanted to take care of one important detail. He wanted to legally change his name to Gerald R. Ford Jr. He had been called Jerry Ford since he was a boy. As an adult, he wanted to make it official. He applied to the judge in Kent County, Michigan. On December 3, 1935, he officially became Gerald Rudolph Ford Jr.

THE IVY LEAGUE

The Yale campus impressed Ford. He said, "Everywhere I went, I [found] an atmosphere of scholarship, dignity and tradition." Yale University, founded in 1701, is one of the elite, old "Ivy League" schools. In 1935 Yale was an excellent private university for privileged young men who were wealthy or very intelligent or both. Ford lacked the wealth. But he was smart, and he worked hard. He was still hoping to study law. He asked Pond to help him get into Yale's law school. Pond said the coaching job would take all his time, but he agreed to pass the request on to the law school. Ford was rejected.

The football team did pretty well that year. They won six games and lost three. The following year, 1936, the team did even better. They won seven games and the Ivy League crown. Ford received a six-hundred-dollar raise. For the first time in his life, he had enough money to save.

During the summer of 1937, Ford returned to Ann Arbor. There he enrolled in two classes at the University of Michigan Law School. He earned Bs in both of them. At the end of the football season the following year, Ford again tried to get into Yale Law School. He was not accepted full-time, but he was allowed to take two classes. Ford again earned Bs. Having proved himself, Ford was at last accepted as a full-time student.

At about this same time, Ford fell in love for the first time. The Yale boxing team had gone to New London, Connecticut, to compete with the U.S. Coast Guard Academy. Ford, as the assistant boxing coach, had gone with them. Friends from Grand Rapids, who were students at the academy, suggested that he call Phyllis Brown. Phyllis was a beautiful young woman from Maine. She attended Connecticut College for Women, also in New London. A few days later, Ford called her and made a date.

The relationship blossomed, despite complications. In her junior year, Phyllis moved to New York City to begin a successful modeling career. She loved to ski, go to the theater, and play bridge, tennis, and golf. Ford had never been on a ski slope or gone to the theater. But, he said, "If I wanted to stay in her league, I simply had to learn." Phyllis and Jerry talked about getting married after he finished law school and found a job. They visited each other's families in Michigan and Maine. But Ford wanted to return to Grand Rapids to practice law, and Phyllis did not want to leave her career in New York. In the end, they followed

Ford's college girlfriend, Phyllis Brown, inspired Ford to learn to ski.

──────────── ✧

their separate paths. He wondered if he'd ever meet anyone like her again.

Ford finished his law courses at Yale in 1941. He moved back to Michigan to take the bar exam, a required test for practicing law in that state. He passed the exam and set up a law firm in Grand Rapids with his college friend, Phil Buchen. Little by little, the firm built a good business. The two lawyers had as many clients as they could handle. Then, on December 7, 1941, the Japanese attacked the U.S. naval base at Pearl Harbor, Hawaii. The United States entered World War II (1939–1945).

Ford was a lieutenant commander in the U.S. Navy during World War II.

CHAPTER THREE

A WORLD AT WAR

*Before the war, I'd been an ... isolationist
[uninvolved in international affairs]. . . . But
now I had become an ardent internationalist.
My wartime experiences had given me an
entirely new perspective.*
—Gerald R. Ford, 1946

Early in 1942, Gerald R. Ford joined the U.S. Navy.
He entered the navy as an ensign (a low-ranking officer).
A short time later, he was promoted to lieutenant. Ford
completed one month of basic officer training at the U.S.
Naval Academy in Annapolis, Maryland. Then he was
sent to the naval preflight training school in Chapel Hill,
North Carolina, to be a physical fitness instructor. This
was an extremely safe naval job. But Ford wanted to fight
in the war. He wrote letters to everyone he could think
of, pleading for assignment to a ship.

Finally, in the spring of 1943, he was assigned to the USS *Monterey*. The *Monterey* was a small aircraft carrier. It was designed to carry bombers, but it also carried fighter planes. The ship had speed and was equipped with forty antiaircraft guns. Ford was assigned to be both athletic director and a gunnery division officer. As gunnery officer, his job was to direct the gunnery crew—the men who fired the guns. In October the *Monterey* passed through the Panama Canal on its way to San Diego, California, to pick up some more planes. From there it joined the Third Fleet in the Western Pacific Ocean.

✧ ————————
As athletic director on the USS Monterey, *Ford organized basketball games among the crew. As an athlete, he* (jumper on the left) *sometimes starred in the games.*

Ford is seated in the front row, second from the right, in this 1943 photo of gunnery officers on the Monterey.

ACTION, AT LAST

The *Monterey*'s first mission was to attack a Japanese base in the Gilbert Islands. The navy blasted the island for three weeks. Then the *Monterey* moved southwest to hit the Japanese on the island of New Ireland. Waves of planes took off from the aircraft carriers and bombed the island port on Christmas morning, successfully sinking enemy ships. "The Japanese planes came after us with a vengeance," Ford said, and "it was as much action as I'd

Ford (left) *poses for a photograph with fellow officer Truman Wallin on the flight deck of the USS* Monterey *in April 1944.*

ever hoped to see." Still, he wanted something more intellectually challenging. The position of assistant navigator of the ship opened up. Ford asked for the job and got it. He said, "When general quarters [a call for maximum readiness] was called, I moved up to the bridge [command center at the top of the ship], and now I felt that I knew what was going on." In his new position, he was on the bridge with the captain, the navigator, and the air officer during combat.

After refueling and taking on supplies in New Guinea, the *Monterey* moved north and east to support troop landings on Japanese-occupied islands in the Western Pacific. It went on to attack the Japanese fleet in a group of islands called the Marianas, where, according to Ford, "we [destroyed] the enemy's forces."

THE ATTACK ON THE *MONTEREY*

After that battle, the *Monterey* joined the ships getting ready for the Battle of the Philippine Sea. One day in October 1944, the carrier's planes bombed Taiwan, an island off the coast of China, forty miles away. They returned at dusk and had just been secured when Japanese planes attacked the ship. Ford said, "The noise was deafening as our gunners opened up with everything they had." A torpedo just missed the *Monterey*. It hit the cruiser USS *Canberra*. Another torpedo hit the USS *Houston*. Finally, the attack ended. At dawn the next day, the ships were sitting targets, and the enemy took advantage of the situation. Japanese planes attacked the entire day. But as Ford recalled, "our guns blasted away and finally drove them off."

NATURE ATTACKS

The crew thought the worst was over, but a different sort of crisis was brewing. On December 18, a powerful typhoon hit. Heavy rain and winds whipped up one-hundred-foot waves. Ford had deck watch from midnight to four o'clock. Three destroyers in sight of the *Monterey* capsized in the huge waves. Ford had just returned to his bunk when he heard the clang of the bells calling for general quarters. He thought he smelled smoke as he moved up the passageway. As he stepped on the flight deck, the ship rolled. Ford lost his footing. He fell flat on his face and started sliding across the deck toward the port side "as if I were on a toboggan." A two-inch steel ridge kept him from going overboard.

Ford made his way to the bridge only to find that one of the planes on the hangar deck had broken loose from its cables. Each time the ship rolled on the wild waves, the plane crashed into other planes, loosening their cables and puncturing gas tanks. Sparks flew. Soon a fire broke out. The engine and boiler rooms below deck filled with smoke. One sailor died, and thirty-three were injured. Three of the four boilers stopped working. The fire on deck burned out of control. If the last boiler went out, the fire hoses would lose pressure. There would be no way to put out the flames.

The commander of the Third Fleet gave the crew permission to abandon ship. He ordered nearby ships to stand by to rescue survivors. But Captain Stuart H. Ingersoll, the *Monterey*'s captain, had another idea. He sent a rescue party wearing gas masks to the engine and boiler rooms below. They brought out survivors and kept the working boiler going. After seven hours, the rescue team got the other three boilers working too. The crew put out the fire, and the *Monterey* steamed toward the island of Saipan.

After the ship reached the island, Ford flew home for a well-deserved leave. Then he reported to the Naval

Reserve Training Command in Glenview, Illinois. He stayed there for the rest of the war, training new officers for duty at sea. On August 14, 1945, Japan surrendered. World War II was over. Lieutenant Commander Ford received his discharge from the navy in February 1946 and returned to Grand Rapids, Michigan.

CHAPTER FOUR

JUMPING INTO POLITICS

Politics is basic intuitiveness. Common sense.
—Gerald R. Ford, 1947

When Gerald R. Ford returned to Grand Rapids, he moved in with his parents. He had no job. The law firm of Ford and Buchen had dissolved. While Ford was in the navy, Buchen had joined Butterfield, Keeney & Amberg, a law firm with many important clients. The firm hired Ford too, and Julius Amberg, a senior partner, took him under his wing. Ford worked hard. He said, "I was learning, and I found I really liked law."

He also began to develop an interest in politics. He had joined a local Republican group before the war. After his return, he became involved in community activities. He raised money for the Boy Scouts and worked for the Kent County cancer drive and the American Red Cross. He joined the American Legion, the Veterans of Foreign Wars, and the National Association for the Advancement of Colored People.

NEW BEGINNINGS
Life was going well for Ford when he met Elizabeth (Betty) Bloomer Warren at a party. She was in the middle of a divorce, but Jerry and Betty began seeing each other as friends. Ford didn't have much time for a social life just then. With the encouragement of the young reform

Ford supported the Boy Scouts in fundraising activities after the war. He had been an Eagle Scout (far left) in high school.

Republicans, a group of young Republicans who wanted to bring new life to the party, and his father (a county Republican official), Ford decided to run for a seat in the U.S. House of Representatives. Friends were not so sure. Ford had almost no experience in politics, and his opponent in the Republican primary would be Bartel J. (Barney) Jonkman. People of Dutch descent made up 60 percent of the Fifth District, and Jonkman was Dutch. He had been the Fifth District congressman since 1940. This meant that he had connections in the House and in the Fifth District.

Ford first found a campaign manager, Jack Stiles, a friend from the University of Michigan. Together they put together a fifteen-month plan. They collected donations and borrowed money to pay for the campaign. Stiles advised Ford to keep his candidacy secret as long as possible so Jonkman wouldn't know he had a challenger. Ford said, "My one advantage was surprise—and Jonkman's overconfidence."

Ford couldn't even tell Betty about his plan. Her divorce had become final in September 1947, and they were seeing each other often. But Betty wasn't eager to jump into another marriage. Ford thought of her as an attractive, enjoyable date.

Then, after Christmas, he went to Sun Valley, Idaho, for a two-week ski trip. There, he realized that he missed Betty and wanted to be with her. He wrote to her daily and bought her a leather belt with a silver buckle. Betty realized that she missed Jerry's company too. The following February, he asked her to marry him. He said, "I'd like to marry you, but we can't get married until next fall and I can't tell you why." She agreed without asking why. Politics was the reason.

Ford's life changed when he met Betty Bloomer (right). She had a career in New York City as a professional dancer and fashion model.

——————— ◇

THE CAMPAIGN

Ford worked on gaining support in the community through some of his school friends and people he had worked with in civic activities. He officially filed as a Republican candidate for the primary election in June 1948. It was just before the filing deadline and three months before election day. Julius Amberg, who was a Democrat, suggested that Ford come into the office just one hour a day. That way he could spend the rest of his time campaigning. At about the same time, President Harry Truman called Congress back into session. Jonkman had to return to Washington and couldn't work on his campaign in Grand Rapids.

In his speeches, Ford told voters where he stood on issues. In national government and economics, he was a conservative. He wanted as little government as possible. He also wanted to spend as little government money as possible. In foreign policy, he considered himself an internationalist. He said, "Before the war, I'd been an isolationist," believing that the United States should not get involved in the problems of other countries. But "my wartime experiences had given me an entirely new perspective. The United States . . . could no longer stick its head in the sand like an ostrich." He supported the Marshall Plan (1948–1952) to help rebuild the war-shattered European nations. He also supported the establishment of the United Nations, an organization of nations that was created to maintain world peace. Jonkman thought the United States should stay out of international affairs.

VICTORY
Ford went door-to-door to meet voters in Grand Rapids. He stood at factory gates to greet workers. He even drove out to farms and small towns. His hard work paid off. On primary

◇ ——————————
Ford's campaign headquarters in 1948 was a World War II surplus Quonset hut. After the war, the U.S. military sold them to the public for one thousand dollars each.

*Betty and Jerry Ford stand between their parents in this wedding photo.
They got married in Grand Rapids on October 15, 1948.*

———————————— ✧ ————————————

day, Tuesday, September 14, 1948, Ford received 23,632
votes from Republicans. Jonkman received only 14,341.

On Friday, October 15, 1948, Gerald R. Ford married
Betty Warren in Grace Episcopal Church. He had mud on
his shoes when he walked up the aisle because he had been
out campaigning just minutes before the ceremony. The honeymoon was short and full of political meetings.

On Election Day, Tuesday, November 2, 1948, President
Harry Truman was reelected. Democrats won majorities in
both the Senate and the House of Representatives. But in the
Fifth District of Michigan, Republican Gerald R. Ford won
election to the House with 60.5 percent of the votes.

Representative Ford (left) chats with a visitor to his new office, Room 321 of the Old House Office Building in Washington, D.C.

CHAPTER FIVE

WELCOME TO THE HOUSE

*From that first day on, I knew I
wanted the House to be my career.*
—Gerald R. Ford, 1949

With a campaign debt of seven thousand dollars and a yearly salary of fifteen thousand dollars as a congressman, Ford flew with his bride to Washington, D.C., to find a place to live. They rented an apartment in the Georgetown section of the city. Betty joined the Eighty-first Club, an organization of congressional wives. Among the newcomers were Pat Nixon, wife of a congressman from California; Lady Bird Johnson, wife of a senator from Texas; and Muriel Humphrey, wife of a senator from Minnesota.

Ford was assigned Room 321 in the Old House Office Building. Across the hall was John Fitzgerald Kennedy, a young congressman from Massachusetts. Kennedy was a Democrat. Ford also met the new congressman from

California, Richard Milhouse Nixon. Like Ford, Nixon was a Republican. Ford and Nixon became friends.

Ford was sworn in as a member of the Eighty-first Congress on January 3, 1949. After taking the oath of office, he turned and looked up in the gallery to the spot where he had stood as a high school student. That was the first time he had seen the House in session. This time he was on the floor of the chamber about to become a participant. He looked back at the gallery and spotted Betty looking down proudly.

In the House and Senate, members have to work their way into positions of power. Much depends on seniority, or how long a member of Congress has served. Senior members get assigned to the most important committees. Ford's first committee assignment was the Committee on Public Works. But in the middle of his first term, 1949–1951, a Republican congressman from Michigan left the House and Ford was appointed to take his place on the powerful Appropriations Committee. Appropriations decides how much money will be spent and what projects it will be spent on.

Another big event took place in 1950. On March 14, Mike Ford was born. Betty had wanted to name him Gerald, after his father, but the congressman was opposed. Ford had always hated being called Junie, or Junior. He didn't want his son to suffer the same fate.

The growing family moved from Georgetown to a larger apartment in Alexandria, Virginia. The Nixons lived nearby. That summer the Fords bought a two-family house in Grand Rapids and rented out the upstairs.

Members of Congress usually try to spend as much time in their home districts as they do in Washington, and they

During Ford's 1950 campaign for reelection to the House, he rode an elephant (right). The elephant's sign invited people to "Hear [candidates] Ford—Potter—Vandenberg."

are up for election every two years. In November 1950, Fifth District voters reelected Ford with 66 percent of the vote. In California his friend Richard Nixon ran for the Senate and won. Believing that Nixon was a rising star, Ford invited him to speak at a Republican banquet in Grand Rapids. After the speech, Ford thought Nixon had made a good impression.

A PARTY ON THE MOVE
The Democrats had won the last five presidential elections. In 1952 the Republicans were determined to take back the

White House. They nominated General Dwight D. Eisenhower, a World War II hero. For his running mate, Eisenhower chose Richard Nixon. Eisenhower was popular with the voters. The Republicans not only won the presidency but majorities in the House and Senate as well. Ike, as President Eisenhower was called, won in Ford's Fifth District in Michigan by 64 percent. Ford was reelected by 66 percent.

This was the first time Ford was part of the majority party in Congress, and power felt good. The new chairman of the Appropriations Committee, John Taber of New York, asked Ford to serve on the Defense Appropriations Subcommittee. This group oversaw the budgets of the military. It was another lucky break for the thirty-nine-year-old congressman.

Ford was good at his new job. He asked hard questions of witnesses who appeared before the committee with spending requests. He always demanded detailed answers. In 1953, toward the end of the Korean War (1950–1953), Ford decided to check on the military situation in the Far East for himself. He flew to Korea to inspect U.S. troops, oversee the return of U.S. prisoners of war, and visit a training camp for South Korean troops. From there, he flew to Saigon, Vietnam, to inspect the French troops who were fighting Communist groups there.

Betty met Ford at the airport when he returned to Washington. She took with her three-year-old Mike and his younger brother Jack, who had been born the year before. About this time, Clara Powers joined the family to help with cleaning, cooking, and child care. The Fords bought a new house on Crown View Drive in Alexandria,

Virginia, in March 1955. The following year, son Steven was born, followed a year later by the birth of Susan. Even though Ford traveled so much, he made it a rule always to fly back to Alexandria to spend Sunday with his family. That was their day together, unless he was out of the country.

A MAN ON THE MOVE

Ford's political career continued to thrive. In 1955 he flew to Europe to check on Allied (U.S., British, and French) military forces stationed there. Then he went on to Warsaw, Poland, and to Moscow, capital of the Union of Soviet Socialist Republics (USSR, or the Soviet Union). Since the end of World War II, the United States and the USSR had been involved in the Cold War (1945–1991). No military battles took place. But the two nations competed for political influence around the world. The USSR wanted to spread its Communist system of government, while the United States tried to set up democratic governments.

Providing foreign aid was one way of influencing a poor or developing country. During the Cold War, Ford took on additional House responsibilities, including the committee overseeing U.S. foreign aid. The secretary of state had to appear before the committee to explain why a particular country needed U.S. aid and how the money would be spent. Ford was gaining a reputation for treating important decisions of national interest in an impartial (fair) way. He began to think of someday becoming Speaker of the House, the top position in the House of Representatives.

THE COLD WAR

The term *Cold War* refers to the rivalry between Communist and non-Communist nations after World War II. But its roots go back to 1917 when Russia had a revolution and became a Communist country. In the Communist form of government, all business, industry, and agriculture are owned by the state. In reality Communist countries often experienced poor economies and harsh repression of human rights. By taking over other countries, Russia expanded, becoming the Union of Soviet Socialist Republics (USSR). The USSR and its allies came to be known as the Eastern bloc. The United States and its democratic allies became known as the Western bloc.

Each side thought the other was trying to take over the world. No real fighting took place between the USSR and the United States, but the two sides distrusted each other. Both sides built up arms and tried to expand their influence in the world. After its Communist revolution in 1949, China joined the Eastern bloc.

In the 1960s, however, the situation began to change. China remained a Communist country but broke away from the USSR. By the 1970s, when Gerald R. Ford became president, the Vietnam War had divided the Western bloc, and the Communists eventually won the war there. President Nixon visited China in 1972, and both Nixon and Ford met with Leonid Brezhnev, the Soviet leader, about arms control.

By the 1980s, the USSR and the United States had made progress toward peace. By the end of the decade, Communist rule ended in many Eastern European countries. The USSR dissolved in 1991, and the countries that were part of the Eastern bloc became independent. By the early 1990s, the Cold War had ended.

When the Soviet Union launched *Sputnik*, the world's first Earth satellite, on October 4, 1957, the United States was caught off guard. The space race, another aspect of the Cold War, had begun. The United States wanted to explore space before the Soviets did. President Eisenhower called for the creation of a new federal agency for space exploration. Speaker of the House Sam Rayburn, a Democrat, asked Ford to serve on the House-Senate committee to develop the new agency. It became known as the National Aeronautics and Space Administration (NASA). The appointment was another proud moment for Ford.

A CHANGING OF THE GUARD
The Republicans did poorly in the 1958 congressional elections. Many Republicans felt that they needed a leader who could help the party develop a new image. Ford became part of a group that recruited Charles Halleck of Indiana as the Republican National Committee chairman.

——————————— ✧
The Soviet Union's first
Sputnik satellite was about
the size of a basketball.
In 1957 Sputnik I
orbited Earth in
ninety-eight minutes.

Ford's leadership in the House continued to grow. In 1960, when his friend Richard Nixon ran for president, Ford's name even came up as a possible running mate. In the end, Nixon chose United Nations ambassador Henry Cabot Lodge. Senator John F. Kennedy of Massachusetts was the Democratic candidate.

Ford campaigned hard for the Nixon presidential campaign. Nixon and Kennedy took part in the first presidential debates ever shown on TV. Television wasn't kind to Nixon. He wasn't as polished as Kennedy. He appeared unsure of himself. In sharp contrast, Kennedy was able to use TV to his advantage. Although the election was close, Kennedy won. But the Republicans added twenty-two representatives in the House.

Kennedy and Ford had entered Congress the same year. They often walked together from their offices to the House chamber. The new president asked Ford for his support in the House, especially on foreign policy issues. Ford agreed to help where he could. That same year, 1961, the American Political Science Association chose Ford to receive its Congressional Distinguished Service Award.

As the senior Republican on the Defense Appropriations Subcommittee, Congressman Ford could speak knowledgeably about military matters. He was getting invitations to speak at conferences and universities. Ford was proud of his record in Congress. He had been involved in many important decisions. One of these was the funding programs to aid Europe and Japan after World War II. He was involved in the development of the hydrogen bomb and *Nautilus,* the navy's first nuclear submarine. He oversaw military spending for the Korean War, for sending the first U.S. military advisers to

Vietnam, and for training the South Vietnamese army to fight North Vietnamese Communist forces. He supported the Supreme Court decision to desegregate public schools and the first act to protect the voting rights of black people.

The one dark spot in his life during this period came on January 26, 1962, when Ford's stepfather died. He had slipped on the ice and suffered a concussion.

THE YOUNG TURKS

Ford looked forward to the 1962 midterm election. He expected the Republicans to win about twenty new congressional seats. For Ford to become Speaker of the House, the Republicans had to have a majority. But the election was a disappointment to him, since the Republicans gained only two seats in the House and lost four in the Senate. Younger members of the House again blamed the election results on poor party leadership. They had a plan.

Four House members—Mel Laird of Wisconsin, Charles Goodell of New York, Bob Griffin of Michigan, and Donald Rumsfeld of Illinois—were part of the party's Young Turks, active younger members of the House. This group wanted change and new leadership. In January 1963, the group asked Ford to run for the House Republican Conference chairmanship. The purpose of the conference was to create practical programs that reflected party policy. To Ford this was an important opportunity, a stepping-stone in his quest to become Speaker of the House of Representatives.

President John F. Kennedy's widow Jacqueline Kennedy (top center) and their children, Caroline and John Jr., follow Kennedy's coffin down the steps of Saint Matthew's Cathedral in Washington, D.C. Kennedy's assassination on November 22, 1963, changed the lives of many Americans, including Ford's.

CHAPTER SIX

THE TUMULTUOUS YEARS

Above all, today's young people demand candor.
No matter whether the news is good or bad, no
matter whether they agree or disagree, they
want to be told the truth.
—Gerald R. Ford, 1979

On November 22, 1963, Betty and Jerry Ford were driving home from a school conference. While listening to the news on the car radio, they learned that President John F. Kennedy had been shot while riding in a motorcade in Dallas, Texas. The president was dead. On the way back to Washington, aboard Air Force One, the president's plane, Vice President Lyndon Johnson was sworn in as president. Ford thought Johnson was a strong leader who could guide the nation through this trying time.

Later that month, the new president called Ford at home one evening. He was putting together a bipartisan (two-party)

Lyndon Johnson takes the Presidential Oath of Office in the cabin of the presidential plane. Kennedy's widow, Jaqueline (right), looks on.

———————————— ✧ ————————————

committee to investigate President Kennedy's assassination. Johnson wanted Ford to be one of two House members on the committee. Supreme Court Justice Earl Warren was to chair the committee. Chief Justice Warren and the six other members of the committee heard testimony from many witnesses. They even made a trip to Dallas to reenact the assassination scene. Ford wrote, "Kennedy had been my friend. The thought that we were reconstructing his assassination sent a chill down my spine." The Warren Commission, as it came to be called, found that Lee Harvey Oswald alone had committed the crime. The commission drafted its final report in

September 1964. The report found there wasn't any evidence pointing to a conspiracy. The commission also found that there were no others involved, as many people had suspected.

At the 1964 Republican National Convention in San Francisco, Gerald R. Ford nominated Michigan governor George Romney for president. But Senator Barry Goldwater of Arizona won the nomination. The Fords sat with the Nixons to watch the convention proceedings. Both Ford and Nixon thought Goldwater would not be able to win the general election.

They were right. On November 3, 1964, President Johnson won reelection by a landslide. His vice president was Senator Hubert Humphrey from Minnesota, who had entered Congress when Ford did. The Republicans lost two Senate seats and thirty-eight seats in the House. When the new Congress met in January, the Republican Party would have only 140 of the 435 House seats. President Johnson wanted to push through his Great Society legislation, his plan to improve life in the United States. With the newly won seats, he would have the votes to do it. Because so many Republican seats had been lost, Ford became the senior Republican on the Appropriations Committee. The same Young Turks who had supported Ford for Republican Conference chairman wanted him to take Charles Halleck's place as minority leader in the House.

Ford talked with his family. Becoming minority leader would require a great deal of work and travel. However, Ford realized that "if I became Minority Leader, I'd have a real chance to become Speaker someday—a personal goal ever since I came to Washington." His son Jack quickly settled the question, saying, "Go for it, Dad." The vote among Republican members of the House turned out to be a close one, 73–67 in favor of Ford.

THE NEW MINORITY LEADER

Ford wasted no time. The country faced major problems, but the two parties disagreed on how to solve them. By this time, the United States was involved in the costly Vietnam War (1957–1975). At home, millions of Americans lived in poverty. Racial discrimination continued, and pollution was harming the environment. Ford established a Republican committee to study the issues and come up with bills that would offer alternatives to the Democratic plans. The Republicans did not think the United States could afford both the war and dozens of new programs at home. Ford's new committee came up with some ideas that weren't as costly as Johnson's Democratic plans for a Great Society. It proposed a less far-reaching civil rights bill than the one Johnson had submitted. To replace Johnson's War on Poverty (an attempt to raise the standard of living of poor people in the United States), the committee offered an Opportunity Crusade. This program would use private as well as government funding. As it turned out, it wasn't just the Democrats who were against these bills. Both the conservative and liberal wings of the Republican Party opposed Ford's approach. The conservatives wanted to do less, and the liberals wanted to do more. With the Republicans divided, Democrats were able to push their legislation through Congress.

As minority leader, Ford was giving about two hundred speeches a year. He thought the legislative conduct of the Democrats in the Eighty-ninth Congress "had been disgraceful." In one speech in Cincinnati in October 1966, Ford declared, "Congress now is a pawn in the hands of the White House, and 50 percent of the members are puppets who dance when the president pulls the strings." Many voters seemed to agree. On Election Day in November, Republicans won forty-seven new seats—not a majority but a good-sized gain.

President Johnson was not pleased with the election results or with Ford's attacks on White House policies. He said that Ford "couldn't walk a straight line and chew gum at the same time." But Johnson had his own critics. All over the country, people were gathering to protest the Vietnam War. Many felt that the United States should not be involved in Vietnam's affairs. Finally, in March 1968, President Johnson surprised the nation by announcing that he would not run for president that year.

The Republicans held their convention in August in Miami Beach, Florida. On August 7, Richard Nixon won the presidential nomination on the first ballot. He asked Gerald R. Ford if he would be interested in the vice-presidential nomination. At that time, the Republicans had 187 seats in the House. They had won 47 of those seats in the previous election. With the Democrats so divided over the war, a Republican victory in November was almost guaranteed. If the party won 31 more seats in the 1968 election, Ford would almost certainly be elected Speaker of the House. He wasn't interested in the vice-presidential position. In the end, Nixon chose Governor Spiro T. Agnew of Maryland to be his running mate.

Two antiwar candidates, Senator Eugene McCarthy and Senator Robert Kennedy (brother of the slain former president), ran against Vice President Hubert Humphrey for the

Ford (left) *introduces the Republican nominee for president in 1968, Richard M. Nixon* (right), *at a campaign stop.*

✧ ————————

Democratic presidential nomination that year. But after winning the California primary, Robert Kennedy was assassinated. Two months earlier, civil rights leader Martin Luther King Jr. had also been assassinated. The nation was shocked by the assassinations. It was also bitterly divided over the Vietnam War.

Three weeks after the Republican convention, the Democrats held their convention in Chicago. While delegates inside the convention hall conducted their business, demonstrators protested the war outside in the streets. Police beat the demonstrators and arrested them. The violence, shown on television across the nation, shocked many Americans. In contrast to the Republican convention, the Democratic National Convention looked chaotic. Hubert Humphrey won the nomination of a badly divided party. As his running mate, he chose Senator Edmund Muskie of Maine.

For a while, it looked like the November election would be a landslide for the Republican Party. Republicans did win the White House, but they added just five seats in the House. For Ford the results were a bitter disappointment.

THE NIXON WHITE HOUSE

To make matters worse, the Nixon administration seemed to discount Congress. Ford finally would have the opportunity to support the president's proposals in the House. But almost none came from Nixon. After being elected, Nixon didn't seem to know what he wanted to do. He had no definite domestic program.

Ford wrote that "increasingly, among senior White House aides, an 'us versus them' attitude began to emerge. If you even questioned their policies, you became 'the enemy' and retribution [revenge] was swift." Ford had taken to heart a lesson the legendary Speaker of the House Sam Rayburn had given to freshman (first-year) members of Congress. He had told them, "Disagree without being disagreeable." Ford felt that Nixon's aides never understood that, and it developed into one of the worst failings of his administration.

In the fall, Ford campaigned hard to elect new Republicans to the House of Representatives. He hoped to gain a majority in 1970. In Michigan he was easily reelected with almost two-thirds of the vote. Other Republicans, however, didn't fare as well. The House lost twelve Republican seats, leaving Ford thirty-eight seats short of a majority. He still could not become Speaker of the House.

THE DOUGLAS FIASCO

For the most part, Ford followed Speaker of the House Sam Rayburn's advice to disagree without being disagreeable. He got along with almost everyone. Ford also made a point of not attacking people personally. But in the spring of 1970, William O. Douglas—associate justice of the Supreme Court—became an exception. Ford had received information that Justice Douglas was receiving payments for serving on the board of something called the Albert Parvin Foundation. Parvin himself had connections to organized crime. Ford thought Douglas should resign from the Court or be impeached (removed from office). Justice Douglas resigned from the foundation but not from the Court. Ford decided to have his office investigate.

On April 15, Ford attacked Douglas personally on the House floor. He said, "He is unfit and should be removed." Liberal Democrats, who admired Douglas, were outraged. They accused Ford of attacking the "integrity and independence" of the Supreme Court. Ford's actions hurt his reputation for good leadership. In the end, the House never investigated Douglas. The Democratic majority voted to clear Douglas of any wrongdoing.

In December 1970, the Ford family spent the holiday break at their new condominium in Vail, Colorado. Toward the end of their stay, Nixon appeared on a TV interview. Ford called him at his home in San Clemente, California, to tell him he had done a good job. The president thanked him and invited him and Betty to visit. Nixon sent a White House plane to fetch them, and they enjoyed a social evening together.

THE NINETY-SECOND CONGRESS

In January the Fords returned to Washington for the beginning of the Ninety-second Congress. Nixon was finally sending his domestic program to Congress. He called for welfare reform, better health care, and protection of the environment. Ford managed to gain the support of enough Democrats to pass the welfare reform bill, but it failed in the Senate.

Frustrated with Congress, Nixon bypassed the legislators. Instead of presenting bills to the House and Senate, he used his presidential power to create the Environmental Protection Agency (EPA) and the National Oceanic and Atmospheric Administration (NOAA).

Nixon also developed a plan that would send extra federal money to the states to pay for local programs. Members of Congress don't usually like to give money directly to the states. They'd rather spend it on federal programs that they can control. As minority leader, Ford not only had to get other Republicans to support the bill, he also had to convince Democrats to back it. He worked hard for more than a year to persuade members of the House. The final vote in June 1972 was 223–185. Ford felt proud of this victory. But he thought he could accomplish even more as Speaker of the House.

WATERGATE

On June 17, while Ford was campaigning in Michigan, he heard on the car radio that five men had broken into the Democratic National Committee headquarters. The headquarters was in the Watergate complex in Washington, D.C. A security guard called the police, who arrested the burglars. They had cameras, film, and tools to pick locks and plant listening devices (bugs). Ford wondered, "Who could have been so dumb?"

One of the five men arrested was James W. McCord. He worked for John Mitchell at the Committee to Reelect the President (commonly known as CREEP). The other four burglars were Cuban exiles (people who had escaped the Communist takeover of Cuba in 1959). Two of them had the telephone number of Howard Hunt in their pockets. When police traced the number, it led them to the Nixon White House. Hunt was a White House consultant. The Republicans were spying on the Democrats. During police questioning, one of the men said they had been replacing a telephone bug that had stopped working. Bugging a phone is a federal crime. The police called in the Federal Bureau of Investigation (FBI). Suddenly, the situation had become more serious.

But Nixon didn't seem to take the crime seriously. He said that he "could not muster much moral outrage over a political bugging." Instead of cooperating with the FBI, the president secretly tried to find ways to defend the burglars. Nixon's aides helped him cover up any involvement in the burglary.

Despite the scandal, Republican prospects looked extremely promising in 1972. But Ford became increasingly concerned about Watergate. He decided to talk with John Mitchell about the Watergate problem. Ford asked Mitchell if he or anyone in CREEP or the White House had anything to do with the break-in. Mitchell looked him in the eye and said, "Absolutely not." Then Ford asked if the president had anything to do with it. Again Mitchell said, "Absolutely not."

Ford believed Mitchell. Thinking he had settled the issue, Ford asked Mitchell to assure him that CREEP would work with the Republican Congressional Campaign Committee to elect a Republican majority in the House and Senate. Then on July 1, Mitchell resigned as director of CREEP. Others at the organization did not provide congressional support. They were interested only in reelecting Nixon.

In the meantime, two *Washington Post* reporters, Bob Woodward and Carl Bernstein, were assigned to the Watergate story. Although the story had the potential to become big news, most people didn't connect the burglars directly to the Republican Party—and certainly not to the White House. But Woodward and Bernstein were determined to look into the story.

THE VICTORY BEFORE THE FALL

During all this, the presidential campaign went on. In the November election, Nixon won by a landslide. But Republicans gained only thirteen seats in the House—not enough to become the majority party and make Ford the Speaker of the House.

After talking over the situation with his wife, Ford decided he was never going to become Speaker. Republicans would not have another opportunity like the one they had had in 1972. Nixon could probably have helped elect Republicans to Congress. But he was interested only in his own reelection. Ford decided that he would run for one more term in 1974 and then retire from public office. He would be sixty-three years old and still able to practice law or go into business.

Six days after the election, Howard Hunt called the White House. Since the election was over, Hunt and the other Watergate burglars wanted to be paid what they had been promised. Afraid that Hunt and the others would confess all, the White House agreed. The trial of the Watergate burglars began in January 1973 in Washington, D.C. Chief Judge John J. Sirica presided. All the defendants either pleaded or were found guilty. Judge Sirica put off sentencing. He hoped the burglars would be pressured into telling the whole story to avoid long jail sentences. More importantly, as Sirica told the press, too many Watergate questions were still unanswered.

THE UNRAVELING

On February 7, the Senate voted 77–0 to create the Senate Watergate Committee to investigate the cover-up. Instead of cooperating with the committee, Nixon tried to stop the members from getting information. But the web of secrets was beginning to unravel. On March 23, 1973, Judge Sirica made public a letter from defendant James McCord. McCord wrote that those testifying during the trial had lied or withheld information. He also wrote that others yet unnamed had been involved in Watergate.

In a speech in Saint Johns, Michigan, Ford called for those denying involvement in Watergate to appear before the Senate committee. He wanted them to testify under oath. Nixon insisted that he had the power as president to withhold information. But Ford, who still believed the president was innocent, wanted things cleared up.

During the spring and summer of 1973, the press covered Watergate daily. Witnesses appearing before the Senate

Of the twenty men in this 1973 political picture about the Watergate scandal, only Nixon (third row, second from right), remained seemingly untouched by months of Watergate hearings and trials.

——————— ✧

Watergate Committee began turning against one another. On June 25, John Dean (a member of the White House team) testified. He said that Nixon had been involved in the cover-up of the Watergate break-in. It was the president's word against Dean's. How could the committee find out who was telling the truth? On July 13, it learned that President Nixon taped all his White House conversations. If the committee could get the tapes, it could get to the truth. But Nixon refused to hand them over.

CHAPTER SEVEN

A FORD, NOT A LINCOLN

May [God] answer you in time of trouble.
—Psalm 20, on which Ford took the vice-
presidential oath of office in 1973

In the midst of the Watergate scandal, on August 7, 1973, the *Wall Street Journal* broke another big story. It announced that Vice President Spiro T. Agnew was being investigated for bribery, tax fraud, and extortion (using force or power to get something from another person). Agnew insisted on his innocence, but he finally resigned in October.

Nixon's first choice for Agnew's replacement was John Connally, a former Texas governor. As governor, Connally had been a Democrat. But he had changed parties and become a Republican. The Democratic Congress, who had to confirm Connally's nomination, was not happy with his party switch. They would not vote for his confirmation. Then Ford's name came up. Everyone thought his nomination would sail through both the House and the Senate. But would Ford accept it?

Ford talked with Betty about the possibility. Since he planned to retire from politics in 1977, he knew that he would never be Speaker of the House. He thought "the vice presidency would be a splendid cap to my career" and provide "recognition of my long service in Washington." The Ford children did not like the idea that the press would invade their privacy if their father became vice president. And they would hate the Secret Service in their lives. Its job is to follow the families of the president and vice president to protect them. Still, Ford decided to accept the nomination if asked.

President Nixon did nominate Gerald R. Ford for the vice presidency. Nixon announced his choice on October 12. That same day, the U.S. courts decided that Nixon had to hand over the White House tapes to Special Prosecutor Archibald Cox. The next day, Saturday, October 13, Nixon submitted Ford's nomination to Congress.

Just one week later, on Saturday, October 20, Cox held a press conference. He again demanded the White House tapes be handed over. That night Nixon ordered his attorney general, Elliott Richardson, to fire Cox. Richardson refused to obey. He resigned from office. Nixon then ordered Deputy Attorney General William Ruckelshaus to fire Cox. Ruckelshaus also refused and resigned. Finally, the third-ranking official in the Justice Department, Solicitor General Robert H. Bork, agreed to the firing. The press called the firing and resignations the Saturday Night Massacre. As the news broke, the American people became enraged. Several representatives in the House introduced bills calling for impeachment (the first step in removing a president from office). Nixon agreed to release the tapes. Ford still believed the president was innocent. He thought that the tapes would clear up the matter.

VICE PRESIDENT FORD

Ford's confirmation hearings were scheduled to begin on November 1 in the Senate and on November 15 in the House. After an intense and thorough investigation of Ford's background, both the Senate and the House confirmed his nomination. On the evening of December 6, 1973, Ford took the oath of office as vice president. Chief Justice Warren Burger conducted the swearing-in ceremony. Betty Ford held the family Bible opened to Psalm 20, upon which her husband took the oath.

Congress gave Ford a standing ovation as he stepped forward to give his speech. In his typically modest way, he said, "I am a Ford, not a Lincoln. My address will never be as eloquent as Mr. Lincoln's. But I will do my very best to equal his brevity and his plain speaking. . . . Before I go from this House, which has been my home for a quarter century, I must say I am forever in its debt . . . . To all of my friends here. . . I say a very fond goodbye."

✧ ————————————
Ford waves to the crowd after being sworn in as vice president in the House chamber in 1973.

A Presidential First

Gerald Ford was the first person to become vice president—and later president—under the Twenty-Fifth Amendment to the Constitution. It had been added in 1965. The amendment lets the president nominate a candidate for vice president if the office becomes vacant during the president's term of office. Both the House of Representatives and the Senate must confirm the nomination by a majority vote.

When Spiro T. Agnew resigned in 1973, President Richard Nixon used the amendment for the first time when he nominated Ford. When Nixon resigned from office, the amendment provided for Ford to become president and nominate a new vice president. Ford chose Nelson A. Rockefeller of New York. For the first time in U.S. history, the country had both a president and a vice president who had not been elected to those offices. Before the Twenty-Fifth Amendment, the office of vice president would have remained vacant until the next presidential election.

After the ceremony, Ford met with President Nixon. Ford never directly asked Nixon about his involvement in Watergate. But the president once again assured him of his innocence.

After Ford became vice president, he and his family had twenty-four-hour protection from the Secret Service. Bullet-proof windows were installed in the Ford home. The driveway was reinforced to bear the weight of an armored limousine. The Secret Service kept a daily log to track the comings and goings of every family member. As a teenager with an eleven o'clock curfew, Susan did not appreciate that

Ford's daughter Susan poses for this photo with the family cat Shan in 1974. She turned seventeen on July 6 that year, her father's first year as vice president.

✧ ————————————————

particular detail. Her father often joked that he could use the log to see what time Susan got in—though he says he never really did.

Ford moved into the Executive Office Building (EOB). He asked Bob Hartmann, who had run Ford's congressional office, and Jack Marsh, a former Virginia congressman, to be part of his staff. Later, he added his former law partner, Phil Buchen. Some conflict grew between the staffs of Ford and Nixon. Ford wanted to be useful to the president. But he also wanted to stay distant from the Watergate scandal. He angered his boss when he stated on national television that he thought a compromise could be reached on the tapes. Shortly afterward, investigators discovered eighteen minutes of gaps in one of those tapes. The investigators said that the gaps included five separate, deliberate erasures. Nixon claimed he had nothing to do with them. But evidence was mounting. Ford began to doubt the president's innocence.

Secretary of State Henry Kissinger and National Security Council Deputy Brent Scowcroft began to brief the vice president on foreign affairs. Ford met individually with members of Nixon's cabinet to learn about the affairs of the country. Ford also met with foreign diplomats so they could look over the new vice president and pass their opinions on to their home governments.

By 1974 Nixon had managed to get most U.S. troops out of Vietnam—a conflict that had lasted longer than any other the United States had been involved in. Congress had blocked any further funds for the war, and only a small U.S. military presence remained at the U.S. Embassy in Saigon, the capital of South Vietnam.

THE BEGINNING OF THE END

Meanwhile, Watergate was tearing the nation apart. On February 28, 1974, the Fifth Congressional District of Michigan elected a Democrat to fill Ford's seat for the first time in sixty-two years. Ford had held the seat since 1949. On March 18, 1974, a Republican senator from New York, conservative James Buckley, called for Nixon to resign. On April 11, a House committee subpoenaed (legally required) Nixon, by a vote of 33–3, to turn over tapes and other information about forty Watergate conversations. By the end of April, Watergate was making daily headlines in newspapers across the country. On April 30, Nixon turned over transcripts of forty-two tapes to the committee. But he refused to hand over any tapes to the new special prosecutor, Leon Jaworski.

On May 6, Nixon heard the tape of his June 23, 1972, conversation asking a Central Intelligence Agency (CIA) deputy to stop the FBI investigation of Watergate. It was clear that Nixon was involved in covering up the Watergate break-in. During much of this time, Ford was traveling around the country to introduce himself as vice president and to hear what people were thinking. They were thinking about Watergate. And many thought Nixon should leave the White House.

The House committee issued new subpoenas for more Watergate tapes on May 15. Nixon refused. The chairman of the committee, Peter Rodino, thought that Nixon's refusal was "sufficient grounds for impeachment." Ford urged the president to supply the information and get Watergate cleared up.

On June 5, the federal grand jury in Washington voted 19–0 to name Nixon as a conspirator in the Watergate cover-up. Two weeks later, on June 20, Jaworski went to the U.S. Supreme Court to get the tapes he needed. He said that the president was part of a conspiracy to obstruct justice. On July 24, the Court ruled that Nixon had to supply the tapes.

ARTICLES OF IMPEACHMENT
On July 27, the House Judiciary Committee voted for Article I of impeachment. This charged Nixon with obstruction of justice. The following day, the committee voted for Article II. This article charged that Nixon had violated his oath of office by abusing presidential power. On July 30, the House Judiciary Committee passed the third article of impeachment. Nixon was caught. He could either resign or face impeachment. Nixon would do anything to avoid impeachment. On the morning of Friday, August 9, Nixon signed his letter of resignation and announced his decision to the American public.

CHAPTER EIGHT

THE THIRTY-EIGHTH PRESIDENT

I have not sought this enormous responsibility,
but I will not shirk it.
—President Ford, 1974

Just after noon on August 9, 1974, Chief Justice Warren Burger administered the presidential oath of office to Gerald R. Ford. Betty again held the Bible. After he took the oath, Ford gave a short acceptance speech. He called it "just a little straight talk among friends." He said in part:

> *I have not campaigned either for the presidency or the vice presidency. . . . I am indebted to no man, and only to one woman—my dear wife—as I begin this difficult job. . . . I. . . pledge. . . to you that I will be the president of all the people.*

He vowed to work closely with both parties of Congress and to work with all nations toward world peace. Then he said, "My fellow Americans, our long national nightmare is over." His speech took only eight minutes, but Ford hoped it would help Americans put Watergate behind them.

Most presidents have a few months between the time they are elected and the time they actually take office. They use that time to plan what they want to do as president. Ford had no time to do that. He had to try to heal a nation at the same time he put together his administration.

U.S. Supreme Court Chief Justice Warren Burger (right) *swears in Gerald R. Ford as the thirty-eighth president of the United States. Betty Ford stands between them.*

The problems of the world and the nation didn't stop for him to analyze them and decide what to do. He had to jump into the water and start swimming as fast as he could.

THE FORD WHITE HOUSE

In contrast to Nixon's secretive White House and his distrust of the media, Ford wanted openness and easy access to the president. Immediately after his swearing-in ceremony, he met with the press. He told them, "We will have an open. . . administration."

As a former legislator, Ford was used to compromise. Working together was necessary to get bills passed in Congress. He was not comfortable with a chain of command from top to bottom. The way he organized his staff reflected this. He spread power to several different staff managers. They worked like "spokes to a wheel." Ford was the central hub, and the managers were the spokes. This plan suited Ford well, but unfortunately, it didn't work. For one thing, the spokes didn't get along with one another. At the beginning, the staff was a messy combination of former Nixon people and new Ford people. Ford needed someone to organize the group. He chose Donald Rumsfeld, whom he knew from his congressional days.

On Monday, August 12, Ford addressed Congress for the first time as president. He had a hard time controlling his emotions. Members of Congress cheered one of their own. Ford looked up to see Betty and the children in the gallery, and he remembered seeing her sitting there as his young wife when he was sworn in as a young congressman. He told the Congress, "My motto toward the

The Ford family gathers for a photo in 1974. Standing, left to right: Steven, Susan, and Jack. Seated, left to right: Michael, Betty, Sugar the dog, and President Ford

Congress is communication, conciliation, compromise, and cooperation. . . . I do not want a honeymoon with you. I want a good marriage." Ford wanted his speech to force Congress and the nation to look forward. He didn't want to dwell on Nixon and Watergate any longer.

ON THE INTERNATIONAL SCENE

Just four days after Ford took office, Turkey invaded the Mediterranean island of Cyprus. Both Greeks and Turks lived on the island. The Turkish invaders used weapons supplied by the United States. A group of Greek residents blamed the United States for the Turkish invasion. They stormed the U.S. Embassy and killed Ambassador Rodger Davies.

Ford didn't want to get the United States involved in a war in the area. He sided with Turkey, a nation that had been friendly toward the United States over the years. Congress disagreed with Ford's decision and cut off funds for military assistance to Turkey. Turkey, in turn, closed U.S. military and intelligence bases in Turkey.

THE HONEYMOON

For the first month, Ford received a great reception from both the press and the public. Americans saw pictures of him going out to get the morning paper in his pajamas. They were relieved to see him as a regular guy. He could be anyone's next-door neighbor. A national poll showed 71 percent of Americans approved of the way he was doing his job. He felt confident enough to hold a televised press conference to share his plans for the future.

But Ford's first press conference unnerved him. He wanted to talk about his new administration, the legislation he would send to Congress, the state of the economy, and foreign affairs. But the press had other ideas. Reporters wanted to know his intentions toward Richard

Nixon. The first questioner asked whether Ford believed that the law applied equally to all people, including Nixon. Would Ford consider pardoning Nixon? Eventually, Ford got to talk about other issues, but then the questions turned back to the subject of Nixon. Ford's answers weren't consistent, so people still didn't know what he would do.

THE PARDONS

Over the next few weeks, Ford talked with his advisers about the pardon question. Special Prosecutor Leon Jaworski was the only person who knew whether Richard Nixon would be prosecuted. He had more than enough evidence. The June 23, 1972, tape proved Nixon tried to obstruct justice. But Jaworski also found other offenses, such as Nixon's attempts to use the Internal Revenue Service (IRS) to punish his political enemies. The White House had directed the IRS to audit, or check, the tax returns of certain people they wanted to punish. If Jaworski charged Nixon with these crimes, the former president would have to stand trial. The House of Representatives had voted 412–3 to accept the Judiciary Committee's report on impeachment. This meant that they found Nixon guilty. But because of his resignation, the Senate could not impeach him. In the eyes of the American people, Nixon's resignation was a sure sign of guilt, but it would be hard for him to have a fair trial. Finding an unbiased jury seemed impossible. The trial would go on for years.

Finally, Ford made up his mind. He called his recent choice for vice president, Nelson Rockefeller of New

Ford faces television cameras for an appearance on the CBS news program Face the Nation. *He announced his decision to pardon Nixon on national television in 1974.*
──────── ❖

York, and top members of Congress. He told them of his decision. At eleven o'clock on Sunday morning, September 8, 1974, in a televised speech, President Ford announced to the nation that he had signed Proclamation 4311, granting pardon to Richard Nixon for all offenses he committed or may have committed. Ford later wrote, "Finally, it was done. It was an unbelievable lifting of a burden from my shoulders. I felt very certain that I had made the right decision, and I . . . thought I could concentrate 100 percent of my time on the overwhelming problems that faced both me and the country." Ford was wrong. Members of Congress and the American public were outraged.

Eight days after the Nixon pardon, Ford offered a form of pardon to men who had hidden or fled the country to avoid fighting in the Vietnam War. The men would not be punished for refusing to fight. (Women were not involved in combat duty at that time.) But they would have to work in public service jobs for up to two years. The program was not very popular. About 106,000 men were eligible to apply for the program, but only about 22,000 participated.

CHAPTER NINE

AFTER THE HONEYMOON

*Politics is . . . the life of a . . . political and
social creature born with a love for public life.*
—Greek biographer Plutarch, CA. A.D. 46–119

When Ford became president, the nation's economy was in trouble. The United States was out of Vietnam, but the war had been costly. During the 1970s, the United States also faced a severe oil shortage. This drove up the price of oil and gasoline. The cost of other goods was rising too. The country was experiencing inflation. In times of inflation, prices keep getting higher. At the same time, the number of unemployed people was rising. Business was slowing down. Companies did not need as many workers as before. This combination of a stagnant economy and high inflation was called stagflation.

Usually raising taxes or cutting the federal budget helps control inflation. But these measures can also slow down business. Cutting taxes often helps businesses. But it also increases inflation. That was the dilemma facing Ford. In September

1974, he created the Economic Policy Board. This new agency was made up of cabinet members and people who served on various leadership councils. Its purpose was to advise the president on how to run the economy.

Ford's advisers decided that inflation was the more pressing problem. They decided to raise taxes for big companies and the wealthiest citizens. At the same time, they cut government spending on social programs that would help the poor. Ford also began a volunteer organization called Whip Inflation Now (WIN). The organization was supposed to involve ordinary people in finding ways to keep prices down. Ford believed that lowering prices would cause people to buy more, which would increase business and employment. Although thousands of people joined WIN, the press made fun of the whole idea. They felt it was mainly a way for Ford to win people's support. WIN quickly sputtered out. In contrast to Ford's approach of focusing on inflation, the Democratic Congress wanted to spend money for programs that would help the unemployed.

Ford refused to admit that his policies weren't working. The November congressional elections reflected the view of the American people. They did not approve of the Nixon pardon. They also thought that Ford had made a mistake in putting the problem of inflation before unemployment. Voters gave the Democrats a two-to-one majority in the House and five more seats in the Senate.

THE BEGINNING OF SALT II

Nixon and Secretary of State Henry Kissinger had negotiated SALT I (Strategic Arms Limitation Treaty) with the Soviet Union in 1972. The treaty called for a freeze in the production of missiles. On November 23, 1974, Ford flew to the Soviet Union to meet with Soviet leader Leonid Brezhnev in an attempt to work out a second treaty, SALT II. The two heads of state met at Vladivostok, a small port city in Siberia. Ford got along well with Brezhnev during the two days of talks. The two leaders even reached a basic agreement.

Just before boarding Air Force One, Ford took off his heavy Alaskan wolf coat, which had served him well in Siberia. He gave it to Brezhnev. Ford said, "He put it on, and he seemed truly overwhelmed." Ford continued, "The results of the trip had exceeded my expectations." But the Democratic Congress soon put an end to that feeling of success. The Senate argued about various parts of the treaty and delayed a vote on it. (Indeed talks continued until 1979.)

A POWER STRUGGLE WITH CONGRESS

On December 22, 1974, the *New York Times* published an article by reporter Seymour Hersh. In the article, Hersh accused the CIA of spying during the Nixon administration on the antiwar movement and other groups in the United States. After Watergate the American public was in no mood for another scandal.

Ford ordered William Colby, the director of the CIA, to provide him with a written report on the spying operation. Then he took another step. On January 4, 1975, Ford created a commission to investigate CIA activities within the United States. The president wanted to take action before Congress could start its own investigation. He wanted his administration to look as though it were in control.

Ford chose Vice President Nelson Rockefeller to head the White House commission. He thought he had made a good choice. But Rockefeller and other members of the commission were more concerned about keeping CIA information secret than they were about investigating wrongdoing. When Colby testified, Rockefeller actually warned him about giving out too much information.

Ford faced problems with Congress too. Instead of the tax increase he had wanted, he called for a tax cut for businesses and individuals. He hoped that this would lower unemployment. He had learned that unemployment was more important than inflation in the eyes of most people. But the

Vice President Nelson A. Rockefeller (left) joins Ford at a speaker's podium on August 22, 1974. Rockefeller came from a rich and famous family. His grandfather was John D. Rockefeller Sr., an oil tycoon. His father John D. Rockefeller Jr. was best known for his philanthropy (charitable works).

Democratic Congress pushed it further. Congress not only wanted to increase Ford's proposed tax cut, it also wanted to spend more money on programs to create jobs. Ford was furious.

ANGOLA

Also in January, trouble was brewing on the other side of the world. Portugal, a country in southwestern Europe, announced that it would grant independence the following November to Angola, one of its colonies in Africa. Until the November elections that year, Angola would be ruled by three political groups within the country. Each of these groups wanted to win control of Angola. To complicate matters, the Soviet Union supported one group and China and the United States supported another. In the United States, a group that oversaw secret CIA activities authorized a payment of three hundred thousand dollars to the U.S.-supported group. Ford approved the payment. The payment was kept secret from Congress and the American people—even while the investigation into secret CIA activities was taking place.

In the meanwhile, Holden Roberto, head of the U.S.-supported group, used the money to attack his rivals. The Soviet Union sent money for their defense. By March Angola was in the middle of a civil war.

THE FALL OF SAIGON

By the following month, the Communist North Vietnamese army was completing its takeover of South Vietnam. On April 10, 1975, Ford asked Congress for more military aid for South Vietnam, which by then was in a desperate situation. But Congress only agreed to provide emergency aid.

On April 23, Ford talked about Vietnam in a speech at Tulane University in New Orleans, Louisiana. He said, "Today, America can regain the sense of pride that existed before Vietnam. But it cannot be achieved by refighting a war that is finished as far as America is concerned."

Five days later, on April 28, the North Vietnamese army began an attack on the South Vietnamese capital of Saigon. Two U.S. marines were killed. Ford ordered evacuation of the remaining Americans in the city. In nineteen hours, U.S. troops evacuated fourteen hundred Americans and fifty-six hundred Vietnamese. South Vietnam surrendered the next day.

Ford told his cabinet that "we came out of a very difficult situation better than we had any right to expect." Most Americans were just glad to have the long struggle behind them.

———————————— ✧ ————————————

North Vietnamese forces took over Saigon on April 30, 1975. By that time, they faced little opposition.

THE MAYAGUEZ INCIDENT

Just a few weeks later, on Monday, May 12, 1975, forces from Cambodia (a neighbor of Vietnam) fired at a U.S. merchant ship, the *Mayaguez*. Cambodian sailors then boarded the ship and took its crew as prisoners. The ship, traveling from Hong Kong to U.S. bases in Thailand, was carrying Defense Department supplies and spare parts, but no weapons. Ford and his advisers wanted to appear tough. Rather than pay a fine for the release of the crew and ship, they acted forcefully. Ford ordered the carrier USS *Coral Sea* to the site. The plan was to seize the ship and get the crew back safely.

The Cambodians anchored the *Mayaguez* at an island off the coast of mainland Cambodia. U.S. fighter planes sank one of the Cambodian patrol boats and forced another to return to the island. Ford and his advisers wanted to prevent the U.S. crew from being taken to the mainland. It would be harder to rescue them there. The president sent eleven hundred marines to Thailand and ordered an assault unit stationed in the Philippine Islands. He also planned a helicopter attack on the *Mayaguez* to retake control of the ship.

When Congress got wind of the operation, some members charged that Ford was going against the War Powers Act. This act requires a president to get the consent of Congress before going to war. Ford responded by saying, "It is my. . . responsibility to command the forces and to protect Americans. It was my judgement, based on the advice of the JCS [Joint Chiefs of Staff], that this was the [best] course of action."

On May 14, U.S. forces moved into position. The plan included landing on the island, recovering the ship, and bombing the mainland. At 7:09 P.M., one hundred marines landed on the island. They faced heavy gunfire from about

U.S. marines recapture the Mayaguez on May 14, 1975.

———————————— ✧ ————————————

two hundred Cambodian troops. The Cambodians killed fifteen marines and downed eight helicopters within an hour. Eventually the marines pushed the Cambodians back and looked for the crew. But they weren't there. A few minutes later, the destroyer escort pulled next to the *Mayaguez*. Marines boarded the ship but found no crew. About 9:00 P.M., U.S. planes began bombing the mainland. At about 10:30 P.M., the Cambodians released the crew, who had been moved to a fishing boat. The bombing of the mainland continued until midnight.

The mission was a success for Ford. The gloomy mood of the country lifted, and Ford's standing in the polls shot up 11 percent. He wrote that "the net effect was that I felt I had regained the initiative, and I determined to do what I could with it." But the country paid a high price for the victory. Forty-one Americans were killed during the operation, and fifty were wounded.

THE CIA REPORT AND AID FOR ANGOLA

On the home front, Ford received a copy of the commission's CIA report on June 6. The report admitted some wrongdoing on the part of the CIA, but generally it was favorable. The White House was satisfied with the report. Few others were. Charges that the CIA had been involved in planning assassinations of three foreign leaders—Fidel Castro of Cuba, Rafael Trujillo of the Dominican Republic, and Patrice Lumumba of the Congo—had not even been mentioned. Members of the commission claimed they had looked into the charges, but there wasn't time for a full investigation.

The Senate decided to form its own committee. It would be headed by Senator Frank Church of Idaho. When the Senate committee asked for White House documents, Ford refused to hand them over. In the end, Ford submitted as little as possible. The Church committee got the information it wanted from CIA director William Colby. Colby's talk about CIA activities and about the assassination plots angered Ford.

On July 14, the Ford administration asked the CIA to conduct secret operations in Angola. Three days later, Colby gave the president his Angola plan. Ford approved it. The president also approved $14 million for expenses. Three weeks later, he okayed another $10.7 million—without the approval of Congress. In Angola the civil war continued.

SALT II TALKS CONTINUE

Since the 1972 signing of SALT I, Secretary of State Henry Kissinger and President Ford had continued to try to promote better relations with the Soviet Union. The goal was to establish international security based on a balance of power. The United States and the Soviet Union would have about the same military strength and control about equal parts of the world. By 1975 the group had prepared an agreement, called the Final Act. Its main purpose was to establish rules to promote normal relations between the Communist countries and Western nations. The final signing of this treaty was to take place at a meeting of thirty-four nations held in Helsinki, Finland.

✧ ————————————
Young Angolan soldiers march in this military parade during Angola's civil war. U.S. involvement in the conflict was not popular in the United States.

Conservative Republicans argued against the agreement. They thought it gave too much power to the Soviet Union. Several Eastern European ethnic groups in the United States disagreed with the country borders outlined in the agreement. They said they would not support Ford in the 1976 election if he went to Helsinki. But the president thought agreement was important for keeping world peace. He left for Helsinki on July 27, 1975. In his speech to the conference, Ford praised the Soviet Union and other nations for agreeing to a "statement of noble and praiseworthy political principles" called the Helsinki Accords. But he also reminded them that "peace is not a piece of paper."

On July 30, Ford met with Brezhnev twice. But instead of coming to an agreement on SALT II, the two men argued. That meant Ford would not have a new arms treaty before the 1976 election. At the closing meeting on August 1, Ford said, "History will judge this conference not by what we say here today, but by what we do tomorrow—not by promises we make, but by the promises we keep." Many Republicans called the Helsinki Accords a sellout to the Soviets. Ronald Reagan, a conservative leader from California, stated that he was against the agreement. Ford badly needed a foreign policy victory before the election. He looked to the Middle East.

THE SINAI ACCORD

For many years, Ford had been concerned about peace in the Middle East. Israel is a Jewish state in the middle of the Arab world. It had had trouble with neighboring countries from its beginning in 1948. The U.S. Jewish community supported Israel. Members of Congress were well aware of the Jewish community's influence in the coming election.

Under pressure, Ford agreed to go to the Middle East. He would meet first with Egypt's president, Anwar Sadat, and then with Israel's prime minister, Yitzhak Rabin. Sadat proposed the creation of a buffer zone on the Sinai Peninsula between Egypt and Israel. This area would be watched by U.S. civilians.

Kissinger suggested the idea to Rabin. But Kissinger didn't tell him that the idea had come from Sadat. Rabin and his cabinet expressed interest. Kissinger then began negotiations with both sides. On September 4, 1975, Sadat and Rabin signed the second Sinai Accord in separate ceremonies.

On the home front, Ford faced personal threats. Within a span of seventeen days, two people tried to assassinate Ford. A woman in a crowd in Sacramento, California, on September 5, aimed a pistol at the president. Fortunately, a member of the Secret Service stopped her. Then, while Ford was campaigning in San Francisco on September 22, another woman fired a shot at Ford. Luckily, she missed her target, and she was immediately captured. Although these incidents

✧ ————————
News reporters and security personnel surround Ford (left center) *moments before Lynette "Squeaky" Fromme tried to assassinate him on September 5, 1975.*

didn't harm the president, they did alter his plans for an open campaign—what he was best at doing.

THE CONGRESSIONAL CIA REPORT

On September 25, the *New York Times* reported on the civil war in Angola. The Senate Foreign Relations Committee decided to hold hearings. Director Colby again angered the president when he admitted U.S. involvement in Angola. On November 2, Ford fired Colby and replaced him with George H. W. Bush. On November 11, the U.S.-backed party took control of the capital city of Luanda and declared Angolan independence.

The Senate completed its report on the CIA on November 20, 1975. It gave copies to the press. As a result of the Senate report, both the Senate and the House established permanent committees to oversee the CIA. Both the Senate and the House passed a bill calling for the end of U.S. involvement in Angola. Ford reluctantly signed the bill into law. This was the first time an act of Congress had stopped secret, undercover action by the CIA. Congress, rather than the president, had the upper hand. Ford strongly disliked the situation.

In response, Ford issued an executive order dealing with intelligence gathering and oversight. It restricted many CIA practices and included the command that "no employee of the US government shall engage in, or conspire to engage in, political assassinations."

CHAPTER TEN

WATCH OUT FOR REAGAN

How can you challenge an incumbent president
of your own party and not be divisive?
—Gerald R. Ford, November 1975

Usually an incumbent (current) president has few serious challengers during a reelection campaign. Gerald R. Ford was an exception. Ronald Reagan presented a strong challenge. He saw himself as the leader of the conservative Republicans. He was not a Washington insider. Reagan had been governor of California. He was not involved in politics in Washington. He believed he could attack the powers in Washington, D.C., and win. Ford supporters worried that if liberal Republican Nelson Rockefeller remained as the vice-presidential candidate, Ford would lose conservative votes. That might allow Reagan to win the nomination.

In November Rockefeller told Ford he was withdrawing from the ticket. Many people believe that Ford asked Rockefeller to step down, but Ford denied this. Ford also announced the resignation of several cabinet members. Donald Rumsfeld, who had been Ford's staff coordinator, became the new secretary of defense. Rumsfeld's assistant, Richard (Dick) Cheney, took Rumsfeld's place on the staff. Elliott Richardson became commerce secretary.

Ford did not want to get too involved in the elections. As president he had to run the country. Reagan's challenge forced him to campaign. Ford promised "never to neglect my first duty as president." But he also vowed to campaign "enthusiastically." Reagan announced his candidacy on

Traveling to a 1975 economic summit meeting in France, Ford and Cheney (right) *prepare on board Air Force One.*

November 25, 1975. By running as a conservative, Reagan sharply divided the Republican Party. He forced Ford to give extra attention to the conservatives.

THE PRIMARIES

Betty Ford was an excellent and popular campaigner. But she did not bend her views for the conservative wing of the Republican Party. She supported equal rights for women. She also supported a woman's right to choose an abortion. Asked on the popular television show *60 Minutes* how she would react if her daughter had an sexual relationship outside of marriage, she answered honestly. She said, "Well, I wouldn't be surprised. I think she's a perfectly normal human being, like all young girls. If she wanted to continue it, I would certainly counsel and advise her on the subject. And I'd want to know pretty much about the young man." Ford never tried to stop his wife or children from speaking their minds. But Betty didn't win over any conservative Republicans.

Ford was frequently portrayed as a klutz by the media. Television cameras picked up any slips, falls, and bumps, and cartoonists made the most of his gaffes. On the popular TV show *Saturday Night Live,* comedian Chevy Chase regularly made fun of the president. But *Newsweek* magazine saw what was probably Ford's greatest asset as a campaigner—the "very plainness of his mind and bearing." He represented the common man.

Ford won the New Hampshire primary election of February 24, 1976, the first in the nation. He took 49 percent of the vote to 47 percent for Reagan. Ford won

Women carry signs supporting Betty Ford at a Republican fund-raising dinner in Newport, Rhode Island, in 1975. Gerald R. Ford was scheduled to speak there.

─────── ✧

in Vermont, Massachusetts, Florida, and Illinois in March. After these victories, the president thought Reagan would withdraw from the race. Instead, Reagan bought television time in North Carolina and won 52 percent of the vote there. Then Reagan went on to win in Texas, Alabama, Georgia, Indiana, and Nebraska.

By convention time, Ford had fifty more delegates than Reagan. But he needed another thirty to win the nomination. Tensions ran high. Then on August 18, Ford won the nomination on the first ballot when West Virginia cast its twenty votes for him. In his acceptance speech the next night, Ford said he looked forward to

Ford and Ronald Reagan (second from the left) *shake hands at the close of the 1976 Republican National Convention.*

campaigning against Democratic nominee Jimmy Carter of Georgia. He declared, "My record is one of performance, not promises. It is a record I am proud to run on." With his vice-presidential choice, Bob Dole, on one side and Ronald Reagan on the other, Ford enjoyed a thunderous ovation.

ON THE CAMPAIGN TRAIL

After the convention, Ford met with advisers to plan his campaign. They set out five goals to achieve through advertising. They included strengthening Ford's human and leadership roles and stressing his compassion for less fortunate Americans. They also decided that vice-presidential candidate Bob Dole would hit the campaign trail immediately, while Ford would attend to his duties and look presidential.

Ford decided that the growth rate of the federal budget should be cut in half in 1977. He proposed a tax cut of ten billion dollars. Tax cuts are always popular with voters. Ford said, "The time has come for a . . . different approach—for a new realism that is true to the great principles upon which this nation was founded."

The presidential candidates were to face each other in three debates, the first since the Kennedy-Nixon debates of 1960. Ford was well prepared for the first debate. It took place in Philadelphia on September 23. He appeared calm and confident. He was declared the winner, and Carter's twenty-point lead in the polls dropped to an eight-point lead.

The second debate took place on October 6 at the Palace of Fine Arts Theater in San Francisco. The theme of the

Ford's first debate with the Democratic candidate for president, Jimmy Carter (left), was held in the Walnut Street Theater in Philadelphia, Pennsylvania, on September 23, 1976.

———————————— ✧ ————————————

debate was foreign policy. This one did not go well for Ford. Max Frankel of the *New York Times* asked Ford about the Soviet Union's control over the countries of Eastern Europe since the end of World War II. Ford answered that "there is no Soviet domination of Eastern Europe, and there never will be under a Ford administration." The debate moderator was about to let Carter answer the question. But Frankel asked for a follow-up question. He said, "Did I understand you to say, sir, that the Russians are not using Eastern Europe as their own sphere of influence and occupying most of the countries there?"

Frankel had given Ford a chance to correct himself. But the president only made matters worse. He replied:

> *I don't believe that the Rumanians [sic] consider themselves dominated by the Soviet Union. I don't believe that the Poles consider themselves dominated by the Soviet Union. And the United States does not concede that those countries are under the domination of the Soviet Union.*

At the time, those countries *were* under the domination of the Soviet Union. Ford had misstated what he meant to say—that although the USSR controlled those countries, that domination was against the will of their people. Carter took advantage of his unexpected opportunity by saying, "I'd like to see Mr. Ford convince Polish-Americans and Hungarian-Americans in this country that those countries don't live under the domination of the Soviet Union."

But Ford refused to correct his error. Instead, he became angry with the media. The error raised questions about his intelligence and his ability to do the job. The White House took six days to issue a clarification. Carter surged ahead in the polls. He went into the third debate, on October 21, with a six-point lead. Ford campaigned frantically. He criss-crossed the country, promising to cut taxes. He spoke until he lost his voice. But a tax cut would not be enough to help the sagging economy. On October 28, the Commerce Department released a report showing that the economy had declined for the second straight month.

ELECTION DAY

The Fords went to Grand Rapids, Michigan, the day before the election. They received a huge homecoming welcome. Ford was still barely able to talk. But he gave an emotional speech to the people who had first elected him twenty-eight years earlier. The next morning, Tuesday, November 2, the president and his wife voted early and then had their usual Election-Day pancakes at Granny's Kitchen—a family tradition since 1948. Before returning to the White House, the Fords attended a dedication ceremony at the Kent County International Airport. A local artist had painted a huge mural on a terminal wall, showing Ford's life and political career.

Early election returns seemed favorable. Ford watched TV coverage of the returns until late that night. About three in the morning, United Press International declared Carter the winner. He had won a popular vote of 40.1 million to Ford's 39.1 million. The electoral count was 297 to 241.

The president was greatly disappointed by his defeat. With no voice left, Ford had Dick Cheney call Carter to congratulate him. Betty Ford read her husband's statement in front of the TV cameras. Many people felt sorry about Ford's loss. He received many letters of regret. One read:

> *You were the victim of circumstances. We all were victims of circumstances . . . . It was a little easier for us to be victims, though; we could merely complain and not be forced to do anything about it. You, though—had the job of beginning the healing. And you did it.*

After the election, the Fords spent eight days in Palm Springs, California, golfing and relaxing. Then the president went back to the job of governing the country. On January 12, 1977, Ford gave his final State of the Union speech to a joint session of Congress. He said, "I told it as it was to the American people and demonstrated to the world that . . . Americans can disagree without being disagreeable."

INAUGURATION DAY

On January 20, Jimmy Carter's inauguration day, Ford rose early. He met with senior aides and cabinet members to say good-bye. He and Betty met with the White House staff, and then at ten thirty, they met with president-elect Carter and his wife Rosalynn.

The short ride to the Capitol for Carter's inauguration was right on schedule. Jimmy Carter was sworn in as the thirty-ninth president. In his address, he said, "For myself and for our nation I want to thank my predecessor for all he has done to heal our land." The crowd burst into applause, and Ford stood up to shake hands with Carter.

After the ceremony, the Fords flew to Andrews Air Force Base, where they boarded a plane to California for a golf game the next day. Jerry Ford was a private citizen again—for the first time since January 1949.

Former president Ford watches a 1978 golf tournament with comedian Bob Hope (right). Ford continued to play golf too.

CHAPTER ELEVEN

LIFE AFTER THE WHITE HOUSE

In a moment of great crisis [Ford] helped heal our country, and left it intact. . . . He was a man of enormous integrity, and everybody knew it. And when the country needed someone like him, he was there.
—Daniel Patrick Moynihan, senator from New York, 1986

After leaving the White House, the Fords moved to Rancho Mirage, California. They were building a new house in the town. At first Ford found it difficult to adjust to a slower pace. Both he and Betty began writing their memoirs. Betty's book, *The Times of My Life*, was published in 1978. In it she wrote about how her physical pain from arthritis had caused her to become dependent on prescription drugs and alcohol. Betty devoted much of her time and energy to supporting victims of arthritis, cancer, alcoholism, and drug addiction.

A SPECIAL FIRST LADY

Gerald R. Ford has most often been the center of attention in the Ford household. But Betty Ford has shown a valor all her own. She raised the couple's four children while Ford worked and traveled. And she always found the courage to speak her own mind. She personally supported public issues she believed in—even if they were controversial. She spoke out on behalf of women's issues and supported the Equal Rights Amendment, an unsuccessful effort to include equal rights for women in the U.S. Constitution.

In 1964 Betty suffered from a pinched nerve in her neck. She spent a few weeks in the hospital in traction. When she was allowed to go home, she faced several more weeks in traction and then many weeks of painful physical therapy. Betty, who loved to dance, had to give it up. She developed spinal arthritis. Only pain pills gave her any relief. Her problems continued through her years in Washington and the White House.

Betty also developed a problem with alcohol over the years. The alcoholism got worse. Combined with the many drugs she took for pain, it became more serious. Finally, on Saturday, April 1, 1978, her family confronted her with her problem. Betty signed herself into the Alcohol and Drug Rehabilitation Service in Long Beach, California. She wrote, "After I came into the hospital, it was as though a dam had burst. Newspapers and magazines poured in, filled with articles about women and drugs and alcohol. Bags of mail followed, and flowers, and messages sent by well-wishers." An eighty-seven-year-old cousin wrote from Illinois, "Bravo! For Betty Bloomer."

Betty became a role model for many people suffering from drug and alcohol addiction. In 1982 she founded the Betty Ford Center for Alcohol and Drug Rehabilitation in Rancho Mirage, California.

She went on to found the Betty Ford Center for the treatment of alcohol and drug dependency, near the Fords' home in Rancho Mirage, California.

A Time to Heal: The Autobiography of Gerald R. Ford was published in 1979. Ford continued to campaign and raise money for Republican candidates. He founded the Gerald R. Ford Leadership Committee for that purpose. He taught political science at the University of Michigan and at Yale University.

Ford and Carter developed a friendly relationship after Carter's term as president. Together they cohosted the first presidential leadership conference at the Gerald R. Ford Presidential Library and Museum. The following

——————————— ✧ ———————————

The Betty Ford Center is part of the Eisenhower Medical Center in southern California.

year, 1983, Ford joined Carter at a foreign policy conference at Emory University in Atlanta, Georgia.

The Fords also built a house at Beaver Creek, Colorado, about fifteen miles from Vail. Ford started a world cup skiing competition at Vail and sponsored the annual Jerry Ford Invitational Golf Tournament to raise money for charity. Politics, public service, business, and recreational activities kept Ford active. He gave twenty to thirty speeches every year. He also sat on the board of directors of several corporations and worked as a consultant. By 1985 the former president was a wealthy man. He was able to live life with Betty to the fullest.

Ford has remained active in his later years. He has attended many significant historical and ceremonial events. Ford, with Betty at his side, was one of four former presidents who joined Bill Clinton at the funeral of Richard Nixon on April 27, 1994. The others were Jimmy Carter, Ronald Reagan, and George H. W. Bush.

In 1999 Ford was awarded the Presidential Medal of Freedom by President Clinton for his efforts to heal the nation after Nixon resigned. The same year, the airport in Grand Rapids, Michigan, was named after him. The School of Public Policy at the University of Michigan was renamed for Ford in honor of his lifetime of public service. In 2001 Ford received the John F. Kennedy Profiles in Courage Award for his decision to pardon Nixon and bring the country through that difficult time.

Ford has spoken out on many political issues since leaving office. He has also come to share his wife's support for women's reproductive rights and has been an adviser to Republicans for Choice. He has supported civil unions for gay and lesbian couples.

President Bill Clinton (right) *and First Lady Hilary Rodham Clinton* (left) *give Ford the Presidential Medal of Freedom on August 11, 1999.*

——————————— ✧ ———————————

Ford's health began to decline in the early twenty-first century. While attending the 2000 Republican National Convention, he suffered two minor strokes. In 2003 he entered the hospital twice for dizziness, and in 2004, he was unable to attend the Republican National Convention for health reasons. And in August 2006, Ford underwent heart surgery.

With the death of Ronald Reagan in 2004, Ford has become the oldest-living former U.S. president. The nation remembers him as a man who served his country and brought stability during difficult times.

TIMELINE

1913   Ford is born Leslie L. King Jr. on July 14 in Omaha, Nebraska.

1914   Ford moves to Grand Rapids, Michigan, with his mother and maternal grandparents.

1927   Ford enters South High School in Grand Rapids.

1931   Ford wins a trip to Washington, D.C., during his senior year and observes the U.S. House of Representatives in session; graduates from South High; and enters the University of Michigan, Ann Arbor.

1935   Ford graduates from the University of Michigan; accepts a job as assistant football coach at Yale University in New Haven, Connecticut; legally changes his name to Gerald Rudolph Ford Jr. on December 3.

1937   Ford takes two law classes at the University of Michigan during the summer break. He gets permission to take classes at Yale Law School.

1941   Ford graduates from Yale Law School, passes the Michigan bar exam, and starts his own law firm with Phil Buchen.

1942   Ford enters the U.S. Navy as an ensign.

1943   He is assigned to the USS *Monterey* in the South Pacific.

1946   Ford is discharged from the navy in February. He joins the law firm of Butterfield, Keeney & Amberg.

1948   Ford wins the Republican primary election to run as congressman from Michigan's Fifth Congressional District on September 14. He marries Betty Bloomer Warren on October 15; wins the general election on November 2; and moves to Washington, D.C.

1949 Ford is sworn in as a member of the Eighty-first Congress on January 3.

1950 Mike Ford is born on March 14.

1952 Jack Ford is born.

1953 Ford inspects U.S. troops in the Far East.

1955 Ford flies to Europe to check on Allied military forces, then on to Warsaw, Poland, and Moscow, USSR.

1956 Steve Ford is born.

1957 Susan Ford is born.

1961 Ford wins the Congressional Distinguished Service Award from the American Political Science Association.

1962 Ford's stepfather dies on January 26.

1963 Ford accepts the chairmanship of the House Republican Conference. John F. Kennedy is assassinated. President Lyndon B. Johnson appoints Ford to serve on the Warren Commission.

1964 Ford is elected minority leader in the House of Representatives.

1972 Ford learns about the Watergate break-in on June 17.

1973 Ford is sworn in as vice president on December 6.

1974 Ford is sworn in as president on August 9. He pardons Richard Nixon on September 8.

1975 Ford issues an executive order creating the president's commission on CIA activities. He directs the CIA to conduct secret operations in Angola and approves more than $20 million for expenses. In September Ford survives two assassination attempts in California. Ford fires CIA director William Colby on November 2 and appoints George H. W. Bush to replace him. He orders rescue of the *Mayaguez* and its crew.

1976 Ford signs a bill ending U.S. involvement in Angola; wins the Republican presidential nomination on August 18; and loses the presidential election to Democrat Jimmy Carter on November 2.

1977 Ford attends the inauguration of Jimmy Carter and leaves Washington for California.

1978 Betty Ford's autobiography, *The Times of My Life*, is published.

1979 Ford's autobiography, *A Time to Heal: The Autobiography of Gerald R. Ford*, is published.

1980 The Gerald R. Ford Presidential Library and Museum opens.

1999 Ford is awarded the Presidential Medal of Freedom. Grand Rapids airport is renamed for him. The University of Michigan School of Public Policy is renamed the Gerald R. Ford School of Public Policy.

2001 Ford receives the John F. Kennedy Profiles in Courage Award.

2006 Ford undergoes heart surgery.

SOURCE NOTES

7 Gerald R. Ford, *A Time to Heal: The Autobiography of Gerald R. Ford* (New York: Berkley Books, 1979), 379.
9 Ibid., 41.
11 James Cannon, *Time and Chance: Gerald Ford's*

Appointment with History (Ann Arbor: University of Michigan Press, 1994), 5.
13 Ibid., 9.
13 Gerald R. Ford, 42.
13 Ibid., 44.
17 Ibid., 49.

18 Ibid., 52
19 Ibid., 53.
20 Ibid., 55.
23 Ibid., 59.
25–26 Ibid., 56.
26–27 Ibid.
27 Ibid., 57.
27 Ibid.
27 Ibid.
28 Ibid., 58.
30 Cannon, 44.
30 Ibid., 41.
32 Gerald R. Ford, 62.
32 Ibid., 63.
34 Ibid., 59–60.
37 Cannon, 53.
47 Ibid., xiv.
48 Ibid., 73.
49 Ibid., 75.
50 Ibid., 81.
51 Ibid.
51 Ibid., 82.
53 Ibid., 87.
53 Ibid., 88.
54 Ibid., 101.
54 Ibid.
56 Gerald R. Ford, 92.
56 Cannon, 114.
56 Gerald R. Ford, 93.
60 Ibid., 109
61 Ibid., 101.
62 Ibid., 109.
66 Ibid., 118.
67 Cannon, 348.
67 John Robert Greene, *The Presidency of Gerald R. Ford* (Lawrence: University of Kansas Press, 1995), 17.
67 Cannon, 348.
68 Ibid.
69 Ibid., 352.
69 Greene, 22.
69–70 Gerald R. Ford, 131.
74 Ibid., 174.
75 Edward L. Schapsmeier and Frederick H. Schapsmeier, *Gerald R. Ford's Date with Destiny: A Political Biography* (New York: Peter Lang, 1989), 259.

77 Gerald R. Ford, 214.
77 Ibid.
80 Greene, 140.
80 Ibid., 141.
81 Ibid., 148.
83 Gerald R. Ford, 276.
85 Schapsmeier and Schapsmeier, 196.
85 Ibid.,197.
87 Greene, 115.
88 Gerald R. Ford, 322.
89 Schapsmeier and Schapsmeier, 200
90 Betty Ford, *The Times of My Life*, with Chris Chase (New York: Harper & Row, Publishers, 1978), 206.
90 Peter Goldman, Thomas M. DeFrank, Henry W. Hubard, Tom Joyce, Hal Bruno, James Bishop Jr., Stephan Lesher, and Jane Whitmore, "How Good a President?" *Newsweek,* October 18, 1976, 32.
93 Schapsmeier and Schapsmeier, 213.
93 Ibid., 216.
94 Greene, 184–185.
94–95 Ibid., 185.
95 Ibid.
95 Ibid.
96 Schapsmeier and Schapsmeier, 230.
97 Ibid., 231.
97 Ibid., 233.
99 Schapsmeier and Schapsmeier, 258.
100 Betty Ford, 290.
100 Ibid., 291.

BIBLIOGRAPHY

Cannon, James. *Time and Chance: Gerald Ford's Appointment with History*. Ann Arbor: University of Michigan Press, 1994.

Congressional Quarterly. *President Ford: The Man and His Record*. Washington, DC: Congressional Quarterly, 1974.

Ford, Betty. *The Times of My Life*. With Chris Chase. New York: Harper & Row, Publishers, 1978.

Ford, Gerald R. *Humor and the Presidency*. New York: Arbor House, 1987.

———. *A Time to Heal: The Autobiography of Gerald R. Ford*. New York: Berkley Books, 1979.

Greene, John Robert. *The Presidency of Gerald R. Ford*. Lawrence: University of Kansas Press, 1995.

Mollenhoff, Clark. *The Man Who Pardoned Nixon*. New York: St. Martin's Press, 1976.

Osborne, John. *White House Watch: The Ford Years*. Washington, DC: New Republic Books, 1977.

Reeves, Richard. *A Ford, Not a Lincoln*. New York: Harcourt Brace Jovanovich, 1975.

Schapsmeier, Edward L., and Frederick H. Schapsmeier. *Gerald R. Ford's Date with Destiny: A Political Biography*. New York: Peter Lang, 1989.

FURTHER READING AND WEBSITES

American Presidents
http://www.americanpresidents.org/presidents/president
.asp?PresidentNumber=37
This site provides life facts and links to videos of Ford's speeches.

Anderson, Catherine Corley. *John F. Kennedy.* Minneapolis: Twenty-First Century Books, 2004.

Fact Index
http://www.fact-index.com/g/ge/gerald_ford.html
This site provides a five-part biography of Gerald Ford with related links.

Gerald F. Ford Library and Museum
http://www.fordlibrarymuseum.gov/
The Gerald R. Ford Library and Museum site provides a wealth of information on the thirty-eighth president. The site provides access to photographs, documents, and information on the Ford family.

Levy, Debbie. *Lyndon B. Johnson.* Minneapolis: Twenty-First Century Books, 2003.

———. *The Vietnam War.* Minneapolis: Twenty-First Century Books, 2004.

Márquez, Herón. *Richard M. Nixon.* Minneapolis: Twenty-First Century Books, 2003.

Randolph, Sallie. *Gerald R. Ford, President.* New York: Walker and Company, 1987.

Sherman, Josepha. *The Cold War.* Minneapolis: Twenty-First Century Books, 2004.

Sipiera, Paul P. *Gerald Ford: Thirty-Eighth President of the United States.* Chicago: Childrens Press, 1989.

Virtualology
http://www.virtualology.com/uspresidents/geraldford.net/
This site is sponsored by the James Monroe Foundation. It provides a brief biography of Ford and links to related information.

The White House
http://www.whitehouse.gov/history/presidents/gf38.html
This site offers a brief biography of Gerald R. Ford with related links.

Index

ABOUT THE AUTHOR

Mary Mueller Winget is the author and editor of nonfiction books for young people and adults. She received an M.A. in English from the University of Minnesota. Her hobbies include reading, gardening, cooking, politics, and theater. She lives in Saint Paul, Minnesota, with Sasha, her Siberian husky, and Muffy, her cat.

—————— ✧ ——————